A. J Showalter, Aldine Silliman Kieffer

Hours of Singing

A. J Showalter, Aldine Silliman Kieffer

Hours of Singing

ISBN/EAN: 9783337376680

Printed in Europe, USA, Canada, Australia, Japan

Cover: Foto ©Thomas Meinert / pixelio.de

More available books at **www.hansebooks.com**

HOURS OF SINGING:

A

COLLECTION OF NEW MUSIC

FOR

JUVENILE CLASSES, PUBLIC SCHOOLS, SEMINARIES

AND THE

HOME CIRCLE.

EDITED BY

A. J. SHOWALTER and A. S. KIEFFER.

RUEBUSH, KIEFFER & CO.,

DAYTON, Rockingham Co., Va.

1882.

PREFACE.

A character note music book for the school room has long been needed by the children of America. To meet this want we present "HOURS OF SINGING" to the public in the hope that it may lead thousands of the children into Happy Songland.

The notation is so simple that any child can, in a few hours, learn to read music in any key. Each note of the scale has a distinct shape, like each letter of the alphabet, thus:

Doe, Ray, Mee, Faw, Sole, La, See, Doe.

THE SCALE IN F.

Doe, Ray, Mee, Faw, Sole, Law, See, Doe.   Doe, See, Law, Sole, Faw, Mee, Ray, Doe.

Entered, according to Act of Congress, in the year 1882, by
RUEBUSH, KIEFFER & CO.,
in the Office of the Librarian of Congress, at Washington, D. C.

J. M. ARMSTRONG & CO., MUSIC TYPOGRAPHERS, Philadelphia.

HOURS OF SINGING.

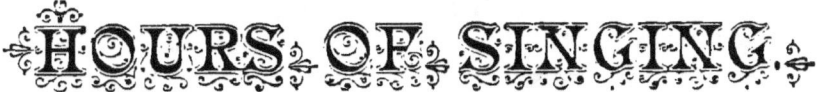

HOURS OF SINGING.

A. S. KIEFFER.

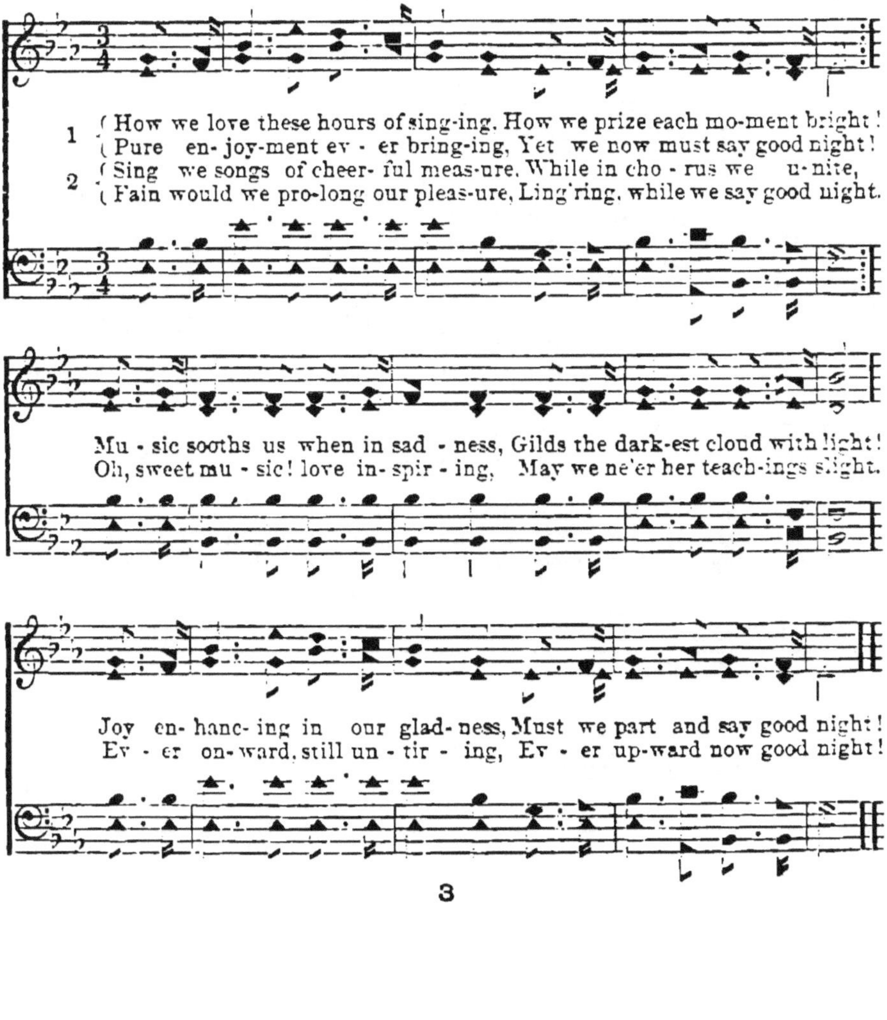
1 { How we love these hours of sing-ing, How we prize each mo-ment bright!
{ Pure en- joy-ment ev - er bring-ing, Yet we now must say good night!
2 { Sing we songs of cheer- ful meas-ure, While in cho - rus we u- nite,
{ Fain would we pro-long our pleas-ure, Ling'ring, while we say good night.
Mu - sic sooths us when in sad - ness, Gilds the dark-est cloud with light!
Oh, sweet mu - sic! love in- spir - ing, May we ne'er her teach-ings slight.
Joy en- hanc- ing in our glad- ness, Must we part and say good night!
Ev - er on- ward, still un - tir - ing, Ev - er up-ward now good night!

WE ARE LITTLE SOWERS.

G. W. L. G. W. LYON.

1 We are lit-tle sow-ers, Sow-ing ev'-ry day,
2 We are lit-tle sow-ers, In the field of sin
3 We are lit-tle sow-ers,— Let us strive to sow

Seeds of good and e-vil, All a-long our way;
May we sow for Je-sus, And some broth-er win
Seeds of love and kind-ness Ev'-ry where we go!

Sow-ing on the moun-tains, In the fer-tile plain,
From the fields of dark-ness, Back in-to the light,
If we are but faith-ful In the work we do,

Sow-ing by the way-side, Good and e-vil grain.
Ere the shad-ows com-eth That be-tok-en night.
Christ, at last, will crown us With the good and true.

COME, LET US SING.—Concluded.

sing, And sweet-est off'rings bring, And sweetest off'-rings bring.

sing,

THE HARVEST MOON.
W. T. GIFFE.

1 Slow-ly where the winds are swelling, Where the sunshine fell at noon,
2 And the light for-ev-er fall-ing, Is a ne'er for-got-ten boon;

Ris-es o'er the tree-top's dwelling, Full and fair the har-vest moon.
Of the an-gels thou art tell-ing, Har-vest moon, O har-vest moon.

WORK WHILE 'TIS DAY.
G. W. L.   G. W. LYON.

1 Up with the morning, Work while 'tis day; Time, like a summer cloud, Passeth away;
2 The Master calls you, Hear and obey; The grain is bending low, Go work to-day;
3 Soon the glad reapers All, all shall come Bearing the golden sheaves Joyfully home;

The reapers are afield, Help them with willing zeal, Go forth and never yield,
    Work while 'tis day.
The sun is sinking fast, The daylight cannot last, Harvest will soon be past,
    Work while 'tis day.
Ye who are toiling hard, Hear now the Master's word, Ye shall have your reward,
    Well done, well done!

A

MERRY SINGS THE LARK.—Concluded.

Tra, la, la, la, Tra, la, la, la, Tra, la, la, la, Tra, la, la, la.

WITH JOY WE MEET.

1. With joy we meet, With smiles we greet Our schoolmates bright and gay;
2. A mer - ry sound Now rings around, And brightens ev' - ry ray;
3. We all will sing Till ech -oes ring An an - swer to our lay;

Be dry each tear Of sor - row here, In school, this joy - ous day.
Our ban - ner floats 'Mid happy notes, In school, this joy - ous day.
Oh, who from home Would fail to come To school this joy - ous day.

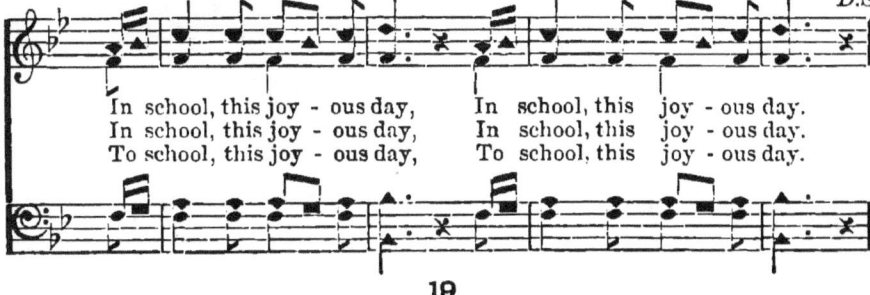

In school, this joy - ous day, In school, this joy - ous day.
In school, this joy - ous day, In school, this joy - ous day.
To school, this joy - ous day, To school, this joy - ous day.

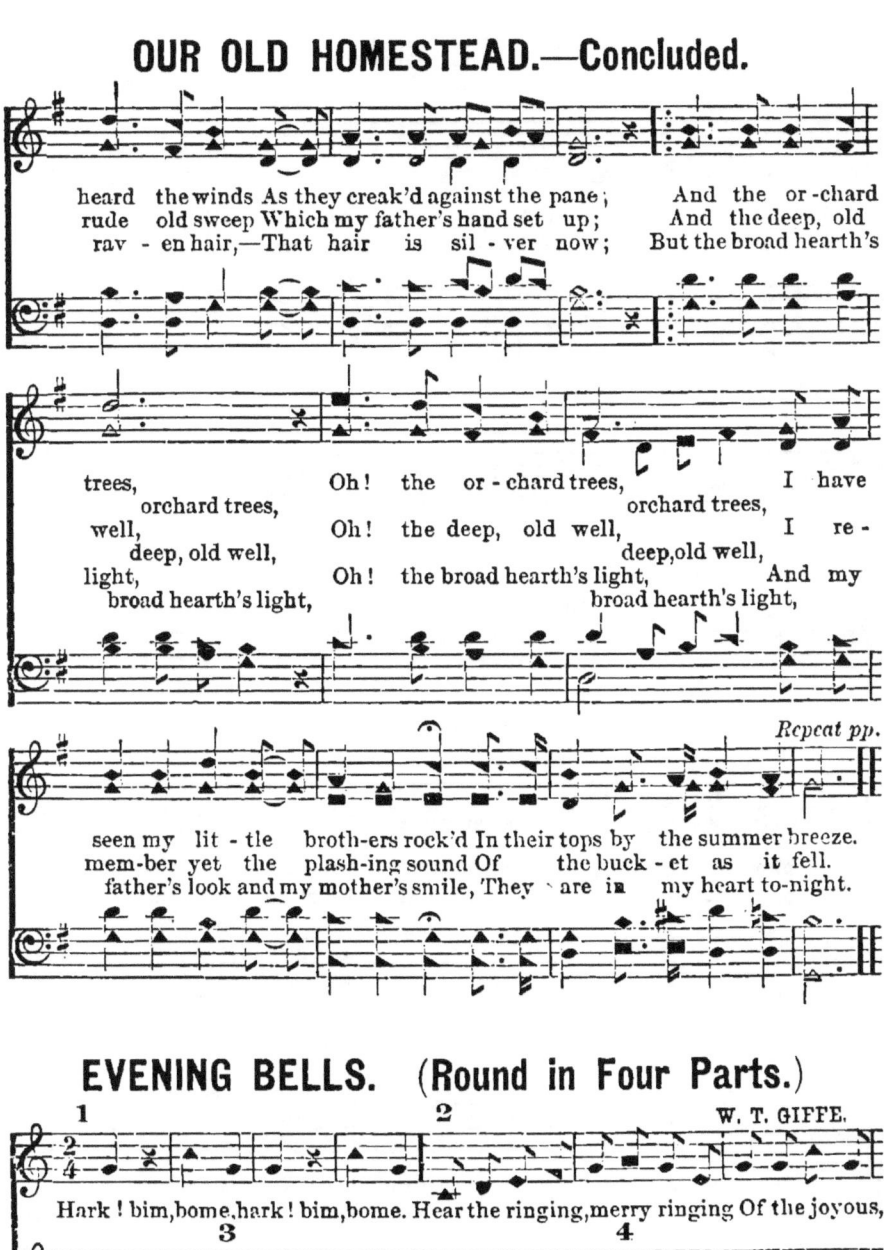

BE GLAD WHILE YOU MAY.

A. J. SHOWALTER.

MUSIC OF THE SLEIGH BELLS.

FRANK M. DAVIS.

30

MUSIC OF THE SLEIGH BELLS.—Concluded.

OVER HILL. (Round in Four Parts.)

W. T. GIFFE.

THE OLD BLACK CAT.

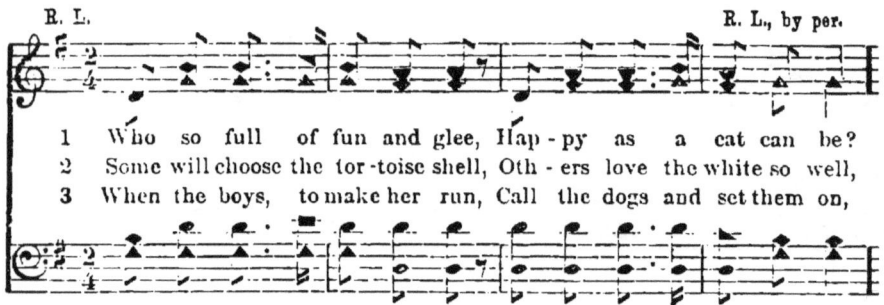

1 Who so full of fun and glee, Hap-py as a cat can be?
2 Some will choose the tor-toise shell, Oth-ers love the white so well,
3 When the boys, to make her run, Call the dogs and set them on,

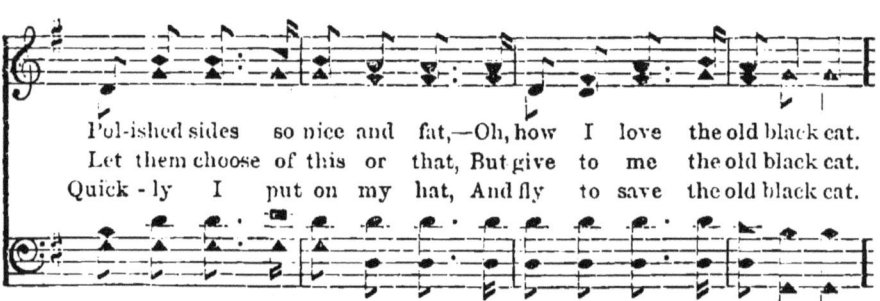

Pol-ished sides so nice and fat,—Oh, how I love the old black cat.
Let them choose of this or that, But give to me the old black cat.
Quick-ly I put on my hat, And fly to save the old black cat.

DUET. *Pityingly.*

Poor kit-ty! Oh, poor kit-ty! Sit-ting so co-sy, Close by the fire.

CHORUS. *Briskly.*

Pleas-ant, purr-ing, pret-ty puss-y, Frisk-y, full of fun and fuss-y;

THE OLD BLACK CAT.—Concluded.

Mor-tal foe of mouse and rat, Oh, I love the old black cat, yes, I do.

TENNYSON'S CRADLE SONG.

TENNYSON.   A. J. S.

1 What does lit-tle bird-ie say, In her nest at peep of day?
2 Bird-ie, rest a lit-tle long-er, Till the lit-tle wings are stronger;
3 What does lit-tle ba-by say, In her bed at peep of day?
4 Ba-by, sleep a lit-tle long-er, Till the lit-tle wings are stronger;

Let me fly, says lit-tle bird-ie, Moth-er, let me fly away.
So she rests a lit-tle long-er, Then she flies, she flies away.
Ba-by says, like lit-tle bird-ie, Let me rise and fly away.
If she sleeps a lit-tle long-er, Ba-by, too, shall fly away.

ROAMING OVER MEADOWS. (Round in Four Parts.)

A. J.

Roam-ing o-ver mead-ows, Sing-ing all so gai - - - ly;

Tra, la, la, la, la, Tra, la, la, la, la. . . .

ONWARD, LITTLE SOLDIERS.—Concluded.

SPARKLING WATER.—Concluded.

ev' - ry son and daugh-ter; The sweet - - - - est draught that
ev' - ry son and daughter; The sweetest draught that can be quaffed, The
can be quaffed Is wa - ter, spark -ling wa - ter.
sweetest draught that can be quaffed Is wa - ter, spark -ling wa - ter.

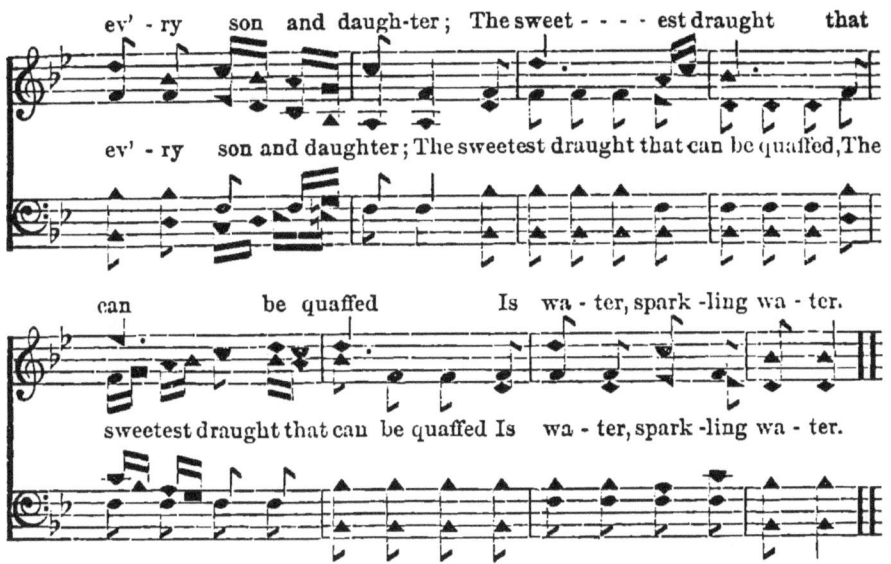

TRIUMPH. C. M.

A. J. SHOWALTER.

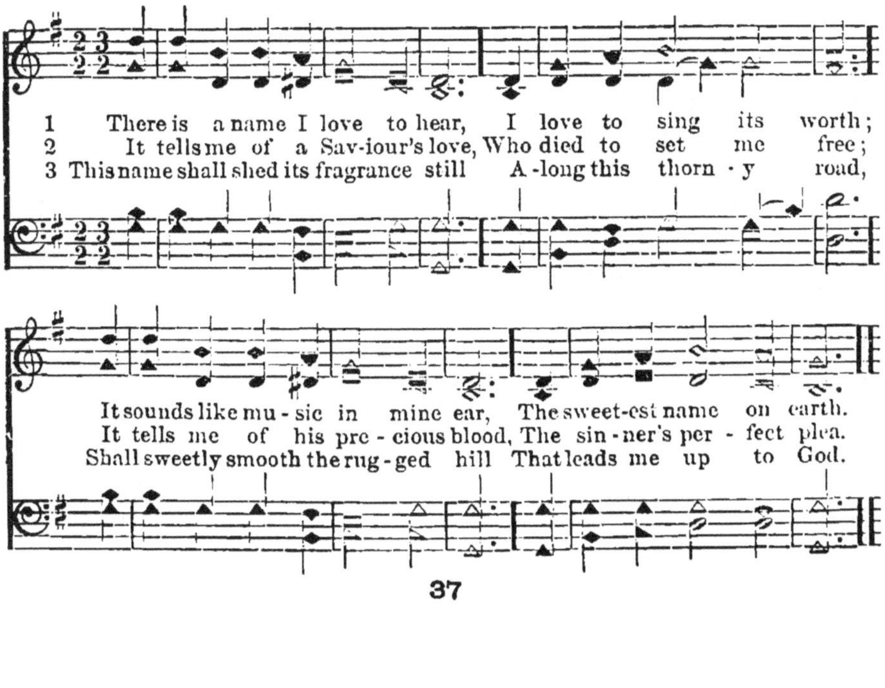
1 There is a name I love to hear, I love to sing its worth;
2 It tells me of a Sav-iour's love, Who died to set me free;
3 This name shall shed its fragrance still A-long this thorn - y road,
It sounds like mu - sic in mine ear, The sweet-est name on earth.
It tells me of his pre - cious blood, The sin - ner's per - fect plea.
Shall sweetly smooth the rug - ged hill That leads me up to God.

WE ARE HAPPY AND FREE.—Concluded.

CHILD'S EVENING PRAYER.

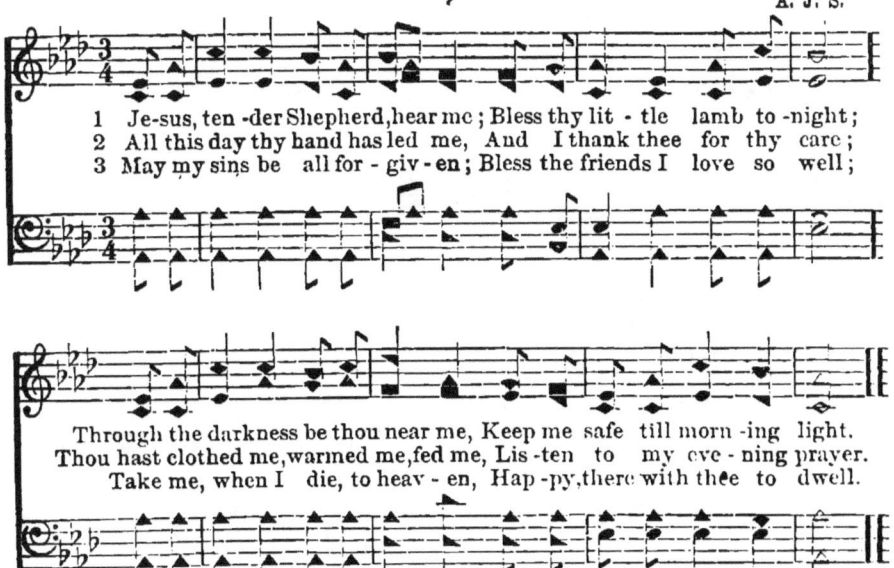

CAST THY BREAD UPON THE WATERS.

Mrs. E. W. CHAPMAN. W. S. MARTIN.

1 Cast thy bread up-on the wa-ters, Sow the seeds of ho-ly truth;
2 Cast thy bread up-on the wa-ters, None shall sink beneath the wave;
3 Cast thy bread up-on the wa-ters, Soothe the weary heart in pain,

Ere the crimes of earth shall harden Plas-tic minds of ten-der youth.
But in God's good time and manner, Thou the bread shalt find and save.
Crumbs of com-fort wide-ly scat-ter O'er the rest-less, seething main.

CHORUS.

Cast thy bread up-on the wa-ters, Give to those who are in need;

Thou a-gain shalt surely find it, God him-self hath so de-creed.

ANGEL VOICES.

EMMA PITT. A. J. SHOWALTER.

1 Hark! I hear the an-gel voic-es, Sweetly sing-ing thro' the sky,
2 List! how sweet the an-gel voic-es, Chant it thro' the si-lent air,
3 Sing, oh, sing like an-gel voic-es, Thrilling notes of love to swell,
4 Christ is born, our might-y Sav-iour, Oh! proclaim the news a-far;

Peal-ing forth the roy-al cho-rus, "Glo-ry be to God on high."
Christ is born, the King of glo-ry, Born that we his love might share.
Her-ald forth the glad-some morning, Tidings full of joy to all.
Still it shines with beams of glo-ry, Bethl'hem's bright and cheering star.

CHORUS.

Sing ho-san-na, glad ho-san-na! Join with them this Christmas morn;

Heav'n and earth re-peat the sto-ry, Christ, the Lord, to-day is born!

CHICKADEDE.—Concluded.

chick - a - de - de, { And mer - ri - ly sing-ing his chick-a - de - de.
A dear, lit - tle bird sing- ing chick-a - de - de.
And yet he keeps sing-ing his chick-a - de - de.

If I were a barefooted snowbird, I know
I would not stay out in the cold and the snow;
I wonder what makes him so full of his glee,
He's all the time singing that chickadede, etc.,
He's all the time singing that chickadede.

5 O mother! do get him some stockings and shoes,
A frock, with a cloak and a hat, if he choose;
I wish he'd come into the parlor, and see
How warm we would make him, poor chickadede, etc.,
How warm we would make him, poor chickadede.

6 The bird had flown down for some pieces of bread,
And heard every word little Emily said;
"What a figure I'd make in that dress!" thought he,
And he laughed as he warbled his chickadede, etc.,
And he laughed as he warbled his chickadede.

7 "I'm grateful," he said "for the wish you express,
But I've no occassion for such a fine dress;
I'd rather remain with my limbs all free,
Than hobble about singing chickadede, etc.,
Than hobble about singing chickadede.

8 "There's One, dear child, though I cannot tell who,
Has clothed me already, and warm enough, too:
Good morning! oh, who are so happy as we!"
And away he went, singing his chickadede, etc.,
And away he went, singing his chickadede.

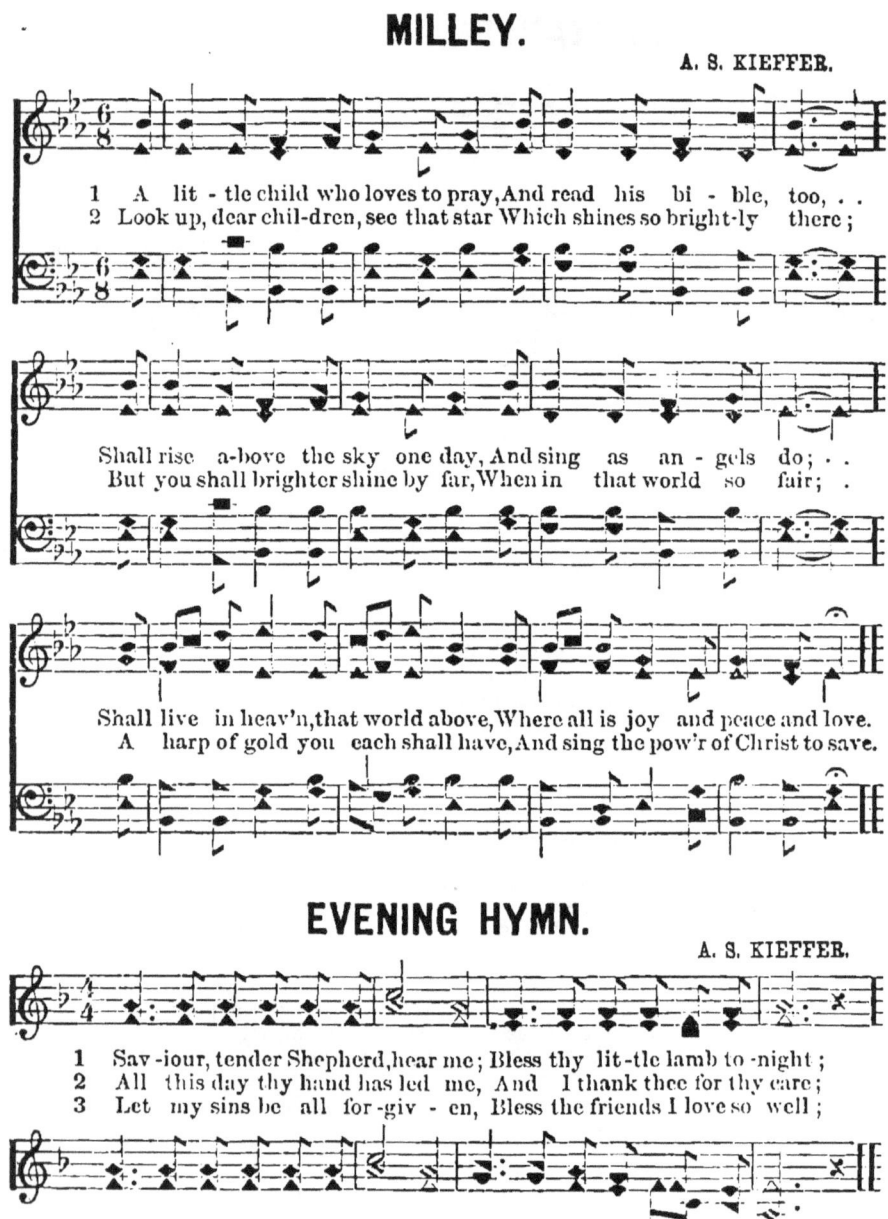

EVERY DAY HATH TOIL AND TROUBLE.

BEETHOVEN.

1 Ev'-ry day hath toil and trou-ble, Ev'-ry heart hath care;
2 Pa-tient-ly en-dur-ing ev-er Let thy spir-it be
3 Labor! wait! tho' midnight shadows Gather round thee here,

Meek-ly bear thine own full bur-den, And thy broth-er's share.
Bound by links that can-not sev-er, To hu-man-i-ty.
And the storm a-bove thee low'-ring Fills thy heart with gloom.

Fear not, shrink not, tho' the bur-den Heav-y to thy heart may prove;
La-bor! wait! thy crown is read-y When thy wea-ry task is done;
Wait in hope, the morning dawn-eth, When the gloom-y night is gone;

God shall fill thy mouth with gladness, And thy heart with love.
Count not lost the fleet-ing moments Life has but be-gun.
And a peace-ful rest a-waits thee, When thy work is done.

BE KIND.

Old Melody.

48

BE KIND.—Concluded.

locks in-ter-min-gled with grey; His foot-steps are fee-ble—once fear-less and bold,—Thy fa-ther is pass-ing a-way.
long as God giv-eth her breath; With ac-cents of kindness then cheer her lone way, E'en to the dark val-ley of death.
love of a broth-er shall be An or-na-ment pur-er and rich-er by far, Than pearls from the depths of the sea.
kind to thy moth-er so near; Be kind to thy brother, nor show thy heart cold, Be kind to thy sis-ter so dear.

GOD IS EVER GOOD.

Mrs. CALLIE W. SHOWALTER.

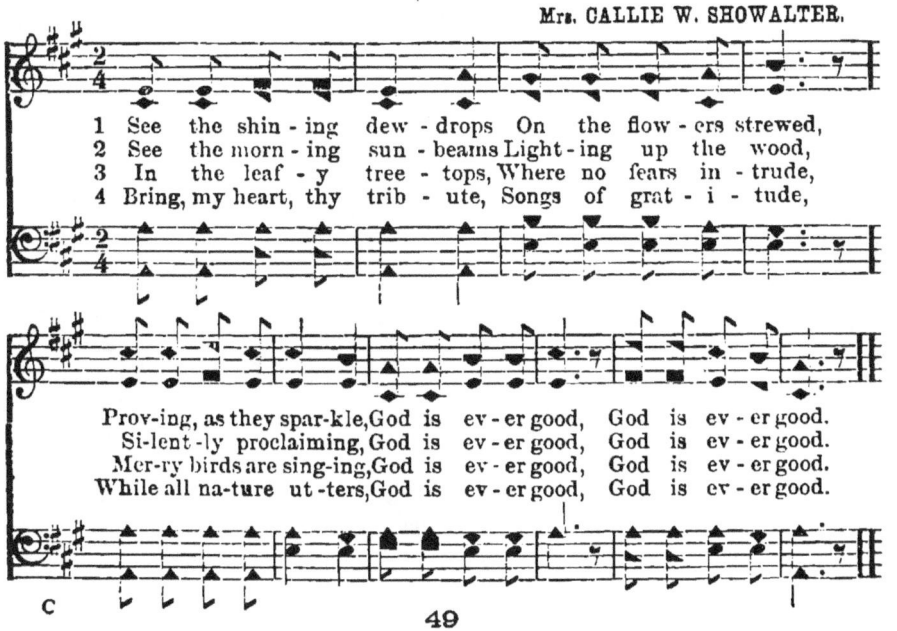

1 See the shin-ing dew-drops On the flow-ers strewed, Prov-ing, as they spar-kle, God is ev-er good, God is ev-er good.
2 See the morn-ing sun-beams Light-ing up the wood, Si-lent-ly proclaiming, God is ev-er good, God is ev-er good.
3 In the leaf-y tree-tops, Where no fears in-trude, Mer-ry birds are sing-ing, God is ev-er good, God is ev-er good.
4 Bring, my heart, thy trib-ute, Songs of grat-i-tude, While all na-ture ut-ters, God is ev-er good, God is ev-er good.

THE OLD CLOCK.

A. J. SHOWALTER.

50

GLORY TO THE NEW-BORN KING.

A. J. SHOWALTER.

1 Hark! the her-ald an-gels sing, "Glo-ry to the new-born King;
Peace on earth and mer-cy mild, God and sin-ners re-con-ciled;"
Joy-ful all ye na-tions rise, Join the tri-umphs of the skies,
With th' an-gel-ic host pro-claim, "Christ is born in Beth-le-hem."

2 Hail the heav'n-born Prince of Peace! Hail the Son of Right-eous-ness!
Light and life to all he brings, Ris'n with heal-ing in his wings;
Let us, then, with an-gels sing, "Glo-ry to the new-born King;
Peace on earth, and mer-cy mild, "God and sin-ners re-con-ciled."

PARTING SONG. *

F. M. LOOMIS.

1 Soft the motion of the current, Still the splashing of the oar,
Weary hands are calmly resting, Longing eyes discern the shore.
Hearts that launched in youth's fair morning From life's river brink so light,
Worn by dangers, toil, and watching, Gladly hail the port in sight.

2 As our feet the shores are pressing, As glad welcomes greet our ear,
Though our hearts are blithe and joyous, Still un-bid-den starts the tear.
Farewell words must soon be spoken, Fel-low lab'rers here must part,
Strong the chain—must it be broken, That unites us heart to heart?

3 Nay, it hath a mystic power; Though we part, it binds us still;
Strong its bands, but light its fetters, None can break it if they will.
Soon again above we're launching, Long the voyage from the shore,
Be our chain in heav'n unbroken, When we meet, life's journey o'er.

* From "FIRST STEPS IN MUSIC." By per.

DAYS OF MY YOUTH.

G. R. STREET.

NEW YEAR'S SONG.*

From "LITTLE LIGHT," by per.

WHAT IS BIRDIE DOING?

Mrs. EMMA PITT. W. A. OGDEN.

1 What is bird-ie do-ing,   As he hops a-round?
2 What is bird-ie say-ing, As he flies a-bove?
3 Bird-ie says: "God loves me, Made my wings to fly,
4 Yes, God loves the bird-ies, Loves the chil-dren, too,

Chirp-ing while he's eat-ing   Crumbs from off the ground.
Oh, he's sing-ing sweet-ly   His bright song of love.
Gave me strength to help me,   Soar so near the sky."
Gives us food and rai-ment,   Par-ents kind and true.

CHORUS.

Bird-ie's sing-ing prais-es, So will I, yes, I;
Bird-ie's sing-ing prais-es To his God on high.

* From "INFANT SONGS," by permission of W. A. OGDEN.

TEACHING PUBLIC SCHOOL.

H. R. PALMER, by.

1 For-ty lit-tle ur-chins Com-ing through the door,
2 For-ty lit-tle pil-grims On their road to fame!
3 Dir-ty lit-tle fac-es, Lov-ing lit-tle hearts,
4 Anx-ious par-ent drops in Mere-ly to in-quire,

Push-ing, crowd-ing, mak-ing A tre-men-dous roar,
If they fail to reach it, Who will be to blame?
Eyes so full of mis-chief, Skilled in all its arts.
Why her ol-ive branch-es Do not shoot up higher.

"You must keep more qui-et, Can't you mind the rule?"
High and low-ly sta-tions—Brought to-geth-er here—
"That's a pre-cious dar-ling!" "What are you a-bout?"
Spell-ing, read-ing, thump-ing Those who break the rule,

Bless me, this is pleas-ant, Teach-ing pub-lic school.
On a com-mon lev-el Meet from year to year.
Half a doz-en ask-ing, "Please, may I go out?"
Bless me, this is pleas-ant, Teach-ing pub-lic school.

BOAT SONG.—Concluded.

WILLIE LOW. S. M.
(CLOSING PIECE.)   A. J. SHOWALTER.

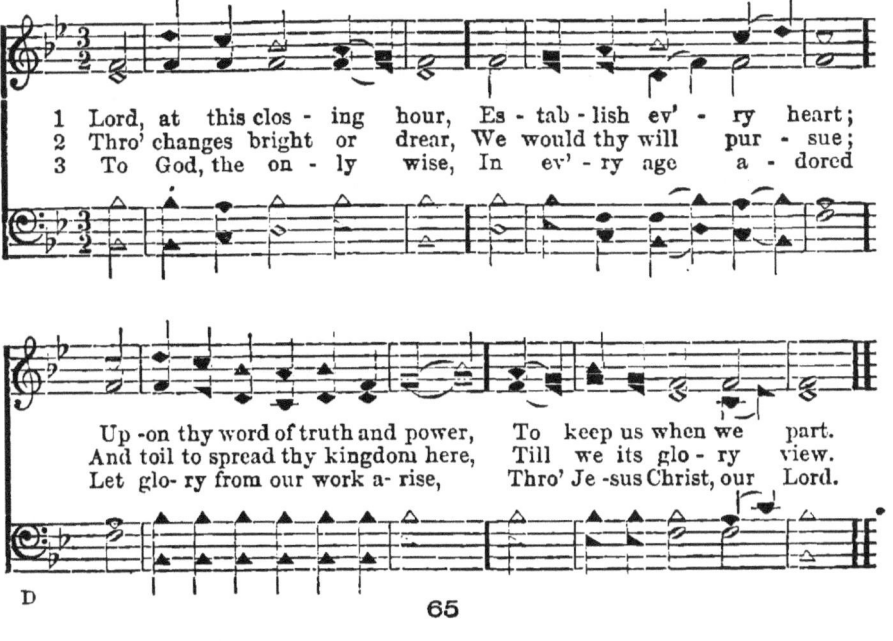

RETURN TO SCHOOL.

Old Melody.

To school and its pleas-ures a-gain we re-turn,
A-gain we as-sem-ble, our les-sons to learn,
Sing with a mer-ry cheer!
Sing with a mer-ry cheer!
Hap-py va-ca-tion, how quick-ly it passed! Hol-i-day rambles are o-ver at last;
Welcome to all! Welcome to all! Sing with a mer-ry cheer.

GOD BLESS THE OLD HEARTHSTONE.

FRANCIS ANSON EVANS.   QUARTETTE.   W. A. OGDEN.

1. God bless the old hearthstone to night, The chil-dren that sur-round it;
2. God bless the old hearthstone to night, With all its gay hopes glow-ing;

May peace and com-fort give it light, And love for - ev - er bound it.
May sweet content and trust u- nite To keep af - fec - tion flow - ing.

May dis-cord nev - er en - ter here To steal our heart's fond treas-ure—
God bless it! and in oth -er years—For time is sli - ly schem-ing—

Nor winds that blow from mountains bare, Congeal our so - cial pleas-ure.
From mem'ry's hill thro' smiles and tears We'll see it bright- ly gleaming!

BRIGHT MUSIC FOR ME.

Mrs. EMMA PITT. A. J. SHOWALTER.

BRIGHT MUSIC FOR ME.—Continued.

BRIGHT MUSIC FOR ME.—Concluded.

JUNE.

T. W. DENNINGTON, by per.

1. What a wealth of ros - es; Fair, and leaf - y June!
   What de - li - cious mu - sic; All the world's in tune.
   Fra - grance rich re - viv - ing Fills the tran - quil air,
   In this month of months the hills, The dales, the woods are fair.

2. From your toil re - pos - ing, Ye of bus - y hands,
   View a - while the treas - ures, Strewn o'er ma - ny lands.
   He, the won-drous art - ist, Paint- er of these flow'rs,
   He may claim from you a part From la - bor's wea - ry hours.

MARCH ALONG.*

* From "SCHOOL ROOM SONGS," by per.

Index.

A little light,	40
Angel voices,	43
Be glad while you may,	24
Be kind,	48
Boat song,	64
Bright music for me,	71
Bye-lo-land,	77
Cast thy bread upon the waters,	41
Chickadedee,	44
Child's evening hymn,	39
Come, let us sing,	16
Days of my youth,	57
Evening bells,—Round,	21
Evening hymn,	46
Every day hath toil and trouble,	47
Father, take my hand,	11
Glory to the new-born King,	54
God bless the old hearthstone,	68
God is ever good,	49
Golden sunbeams,	53
Happy are we,	42
Happy home,	51
Happy new year,—Round,	12
Hours of singing,	3
It is better to whistle than whine,	62
June,	74
Little children's song,	27
Little Tot,	63
Live for something,	70
Lo! the glad morn,	28
Marching along,	75
Merry sings the lark,	18
Milley,	46
Morning hymn,	78
Music of the sleigh bells,	30
New year's song,	58

O'er the sea,	5
Old winter,	15
Onward, little soldiers,	34
Our old homestead,	20
Our parting song,	25
Over hill,—Round,	31
Parting,	23
Parting song,	55
Picnic song,	22
Return to school,	67
Ring the bells,	29
Roaming over meadows,—Round,	33
Seedtime and harvest,	56
Sing us a song, birdie,	26
Snowflakes are falling—Round,	26
Sowing the seed,	12
Sparkling water,	36
Spring song,	4
Sun shower,	8
Supplication,—7s,	7
Sweet summer rain,	76
Teaching public school,	60
Tennyson's cradle song,	33
The dream of home,	66
The fairies,	13
The harvest moon,	17
The lark is soaring high,	52
The merry bugle calls,	10
The old black cat,	32
The old clock,	50
The old farm gate,	61
Touch me gently, Time,	69
Triumph,—C. M.	37
We are happy and free,	38
We are little sowers,	14
What is birdie doing?	59
Willie Low—S. M.	65
With joy we meet,	19
Work while the day lasts,	6
Work while 'tis day,	17

Music Typography by

J. M. ARMSTRONG & CO.,

710 Sansom Street, Philadelphia, Pa.

www.ingramcontent.com/pod-product-compliance
Lightning Source LLC
Chambersburg PA
CBHW031608110426
42742CB00037B/1333